Anchored *in* LOVE

Marlene Lennox

ISBN 979-8-88685-695-8 (paperback)
ISBN 979-8-88685-696-5 (digital)

Christian Faith Publishing
832 Park Avenue
Meadville, PA 16335
www.christianfaithpublishing.com

Printed in the United States of America

Lennox
East
Forty years of
fashion, fun and
all the love a
heart can hold.

Contents

Acknowledgments vii
1. Thank You, God 1
2. Every Day Is a Beautiful Day 2
3. My Life a Blessing........... 3
4. If You Could See............. 4
5. Let Us Be Thankful......... 5
6. Undeserving 6
7. It's All About the Love 7
8. Love 9
9. Wedding Day.................10
10. Mommy Number Two....11
11. God's Gift....................13
12. Living in Love.................14
13. After the Storm.................16
14. A Sudden Storm 17
15. Summer '98 19
16. God's Love....................20
17. To Every Soldier 21
18. A Memory on Mother's Day..................22
19. To a Teenager from His Mother...................23
20. Mother's Love 24
21. On Father's Day.............25
22. A Message from a Father in Heaven 27
23. Pastor 28
24. Drummondtown Community Church 30
25. Easter Sunday 31
26. Thanksgiving..................33
27. Christmas 34
28. How Can I Have Christmas?.....................35
29. There'll Always Be a Song..............................36
30. To Pap Rayner 37
31. My Prayer for Pappy Lennox..................38
32. To Mammaw and Pappy 39
33. God Made Great Beauty.........................41
34. To All Mothers 42
35. Young Love....................43
36. You're the Reason...........45
37. Anniversary 46
38. New Baby.......................47
39. Little Cottage 48
40. Blessing 49
41. Garter.............................50
42. Seamstress......................51
43. Music Lessons................52
44. A Queen without a Crown 53
45. To Louie.........................55
46. I Wonder 56
47. It's Time 58

Acknowledgments

This book is dedicated to my dearest friend, Lou Bittinger. Without her, I would have lost all of my memories. She has organized and arranged everyone. For years I had hidden and tucked away all of it. Lou took on this challenge. I know she found crumpled-up papers in my dresser drawers, magazines, books, and even my Bible. I know she spent countless hours accomplishing this precious gift for me. I treasure her love and this gift.

A special thank-you to Aaron Long and Charlene Lennox for designing the front cover.

And a special thanks to all my family and friends for their love and inspiration for this project.

Thank You, God

Thank you, God, for forgiving when I forgot
Thank you, God, for giving when I did not
Thank you, God, for blessings I did not deserve
Thank you, God, for others when I did not serve
Thank you, God, for loving, a worthless fool like me
Thank you, God, for watching when I did not see
Thank you, God, for hearing, when my ears were closed in sin
Thank you, God, for cleansing a heart so dark within
Thank you, God, for everything, your love has proved to me
Forgiving me for all I was, when you knew what I should be
Help me, God, to do all things, your will in every day
Help me, Lord, to follow you, in each and every way
Yes, thank you, God, for everything my lips could never tell
The precious gift you gave for me to save my soul from hell
O God, I come to you with a grateful humble heart
For your mercies granted me right from the very start
Now let me live this life for you
To show your love in all I do, in any way to do my part
Till Jesus lives in every heart.

Every Day Is a Beautiful Day

Every day is a Beautiful Day a gift from God above

Every day is a Beautiful Day if your heart is full of love

Every day is a Beautiful Day every day is a test

Every day is a Beautiful Day if you have done your best

Every day is a Beautiful Day each different from the other

Every day is a Beautiful Day if you have loved a sister or brother

Every day is a Beautiful Day to share the
blessings that you have known

Every day is a Beautiful Day to be in his family never alone

Every day is a Beautiful Day to treasure the time savor the way

Every day is a Beautiful Day Free without price no cost to pay

So take each Beautiful Day as a gift from the Father above

Make it Beautiful for someone and fill it with love

Then somebody somewhere from your love will say

Every day is a Beautiful Day

My Life a Blessing

Lord, let my life be a blessing; Lord, let it glorify you
Lord, make my life be a blessing, in everything that I say and do.

Lord, let the things that I wish for be for all things above
May the gifts that I give reflect only you and your love.

May the roads that I travel, in this life below
Be pathways for others to follow, from seeds that I sow.

Let the words that I speak be words to reveal
That your love can save, that your love will heal.

Let the deeds that I do be deeds that show others
That all on the earth are my sisters and brothers.

To you, we are all equal, regardless of the kind
We are one in love's body, one spirit, one mind.

Alone we are nothing, not one thing can we do
Till we kneel at the cross and give our life to you.

Then you can make us become, what you want us to be
Make each life a mirror, for the sinner to see.

That your word is holy, that your word is true
That you take all things broken, and make them all new.

That love conquers all, puts an end to all strife
Gives us peace, hope and joy, and eternal life.

If You Could See

If you could see into my heart, then you could clearly see
The love that lives there, just as real as it is meant to be
A love that gives me the courage and faith to carry on
To a day that's coming soon, that will bring a fresh new dawn
My peace is in his promise, my hope is in his word.
Of mansions fair that eyes have never seen or ears have ever heard
So I have no question, a debate, or a doubt
My heart's full of his love, and I'm never without
The peace of his presence surrounds me with love
Assures me of heaven, and my home up above
So don't see me sad, look at me blessed
I've known the rare treasure of real happiness
God's word is my promise, I'll abandon it never
His love never fails, and our love lives forever.

Let Us Be Thankful

Let us be thankful for everyday things.
For sunrise in the morning and the light that it brings.

Let us be thankful for each day we live.
For blessings or burdens that each day will give.

Let us be thankful for a world that abounds.
With beauty and wonder, with stillness and sounds.

Let us be thankful for family and friends.
For love has no limits and love has no end.

For each life is chosen and given by God.
To be lived in his presence as homeward we trod.

As we are winding down this journey below.
We can trust in the master as he'll let us know.

It's only the beginning; the best yet will be.
Our future was secured at Calvary.

For a savior called Jesus who hung on the tree.
To give life everlasting to you and me.

So forever be thankful for God and his love.
And the new home he has waiting in heaven above.

Undeserving

So small and insignificant, so minute and undeserving.
Help us to understand and learn of the
mighty God we should be serving.
The God who rules the universe and created the mighty sea.
The God who sends the wind and rain yet
takes thought of you and me.
How vast his arm that reaches down to creatures here below.
Who most times rarely think of him or take the time to know?
How great he is, how awesome is the work of his creations.
The beauty of the worlds he made, his blessings to all nations.
How mindless, we like misbehaving, thoughtless children, be
Who never give him praise or recognize
the honor due to his sovereignty?
Yet, he looks down with his great love and pities each and every one
Who learns from him and will not accept
the gift of his begotten son?
The son he sent from Glory and from heavens majesty
To suffer and to die for all of us and a lonely hill called Calvary
What love, what wondrous love we cannot begin to know
Until we open up our hearts and let his love within us grow
Help us, God, to recognize your wonder and your power
Help us, Lord, to serve you and fear the lateness of the hour
For time is winding down and coming is the day
When we will stand and give account for
all we've done along our way.
Help us, Lord, to see it now, to fall on our bended knees
To know that you and you alone control each destiny
But most of all to thank you, whoever we may be
For letting us undeserving ones live with you, throughout eternity.

It's All About the Love

It's not about the money
It's all about the love

It's not about success or fame
It's not about the rules
It's not about the game we play
with diamonds, cars, or jewels

It's not about your neighborhood
Or the street on which you live
It's not about your assets
But the gifts you have to give

It's not about the manager
It's not about the boss
It's not about the bottom line
The profit or the loss

It's all about a savior
And it's all about his cross

It's not about the silver
It's not about the gold
It's all about his story
And that it must be told

It's not about the president
Or who is the CEO
It's all about the king of kings
And do you really know

That he's the one who died for us
And forever is the same
It's all about his love for us
And it's all about his name

It's not about this world below
It's about the world above
It's all about us getting there
Where it's all about the love

Love

God says love is a gift, always patient and kind
Love fills the heart and renews the mind
Love is all powerful, all cleansing, all true
There's not a force or fear love doesn't breakthrough
Love is all faithful; you're never alone
Its power and its promise are never outgrown
Its beauty and brightness are never out shown
Love doesn't boast, love will always rejoice
Love speaks of truth with a soft gentle voice
Love doesn't abandon, love never leaves
Love doesn't question, love always believes
Love hopes all things and endures all stormy weather
For life is for a season, but love is forever
For nothing on earth or heaven above
Holds the wonder or beauty of two people in love
So regardless of the heights we may reach or depths we may fall
Love is our most precious gift and is given to all
Given to us from the Father above
So we may know him through the gift of his love

Wedding Day

It doesn't matter what the people think,
It doesn't matter what they say
It only matters that today starts
forever, on your wedding day.
A lifetime to cherish and thank God above.
Who gives you the gift of his wondrous love
You don't need a group, an
assembly, or a crowd.

You don't have to whisper or shout it out loud.
For God of the universe has given to you
A love everlasting to carry you through.
You know in your hearts
That this love can't be shaken
This love can't be broken, divided, or taken.
This love is so strong, yet so gentle and true
This love is so priceless, yet freely given to you.
This love is ageless, and time doesn't matter
This love is forever, and nothing can shatter.
This love doesn't measure the distance; it doesn't count miles.
This love measures in service and counts only the smiles.
This love is so different, so precious, and rare.
God gives to the few who are willing to share.
And all who know him, share your joy, and give God the Glory.
They all know God has written, another love story.
This love knows nothing can change; it's forever the same.
Because God has sealed and blessed in his name.
This love knows only the future, never remembers the past.
This love only grows deeper and always will last.
So look up to heaven; this love cannot end.
God has given you your soulmate, your lover, your friend.

Mommy Number Two

(From a Grandmother)

She was so rare and beautiful, but her work on earth was done.
The angels came and carried home, your Mommy Number One.
She did not want to leave us; she did not choose to go.
How very much she loved us, only God and heaven know,
But God alone is sovereign, and we know it was his command,
To leave us here, and take her there, and put you in my hand.
"Oh god," I cried, "This can't be true. I don't know what to do."
Be still my child, he softly said, "You will
be their Mommy Number Two."
Sometimes the sunshine wasn't there, and
the skies weren't always blue.
But we lived and loved knowing no matter what,
I was only Mommy Number Two.
We both knew she'd always be your mommy,
and I never could replace.
Her tenderness, her gentleness, or the beauty on her face.
It wasn't always easy; I'm sure it seemed hard on you.
But with God and love beside us, we always made it through.
The deepest grief a soul can know was forced on me and you.
As I struggled and stumbled, learning to
be your Mommy Number Two.
We did not travel this road alone; her spirit was always here,
Her love calmed our troubled hearts and chased away our fear.
We laughed and we cried; we prayed and we tried.
We were bonded in grief, but we were grounded in love,
Our family was shattered but held together by God up above.
Sometimes the day was endless, and the nights were very long.
But love and Jesus kept us, and we would always sing our song.

A song of strength and wisdom, melodies of love.
We know it was our message from someone up above.
I can't believe we've come this far; there are no words to say.
The love and pride that fills my heart on this, your wedding day.
Still, we know in our hearts this is part of God's plan,
He knew it was only for you when he created this man.
A man so good and handsome, a man so gentle and true.
He'll love you and protect you, as all good husbands do.
Your beauty leaves me speechless on this special day.
In your sweet smile, I catch a glimpse of
someone, very close yet very far away
Someone who loves you dearly and is so very proud of you.
Someone who was always with us, in all we had to do.
Someone who knows we give God the
glory; we praise him and his son.
We are so thankful and so grateful; great things they have done!
We know this is the path for us; we know how blessed we are.
We know she waits and watches, behind the brightest star.
I've loved you so long now, held you most precious and dear.
The greatest joy in all my life was caring
for you, and having you near.
I am so very proud of you and the woman you have grown to be.
A woman of God, a woman of love, full of grace and dignity.
I know we will be together one day, in a home beyond the sun.
Our family and loved ones, you, and me. And
Jesus and Mommy Number One.
I know I can step back now; there is little left
to do, except to say, "I love you," and
"I thank you," for allowing me to be your Mommy Number Two!

God's Gift

God gave me a gift, a most precious gift;
it was mine to hold for a season.
God reclaimed my gift, away from my sight,
not letting me know his reason.
I know I should not question, what I cannot understand.
I know the Father works all good to complete his master plan.
So now would I rather I'd never tasted.
The sweet nectar of love that to some may seem wasted.
Would it be better yet to have not known its pleasure?
Can a gift that is taken still remain mine to treasure.
From the depth of my being, there are no words to relate.
The loss or the heartache, that now is my fate.
This sorrow surrounds me in waves of despair.
Yet all of this now can never compare.
To the joy that was mine and the life, we did share.
For the love that you gave me, as well can't be told.
Not measured or traded or borrowed or sold.
It's mine still to have; it's still mine still to hold.
It's mine still to treasure, more precious than gold.
It's mine still as real, still as tried, still as true.
For now and forever, I will always love you.
So the pain of the parting and all that it cost
Has still all been worth it, as love never lost?
For God's gift of love can never depart.
It lives on forever in the soul of my heart.
So forever I'm thankful and gave God the glory
That my precious gift was his greatest love story.

Living in Love

I've climbed up life's mountains; I've known some valleys below.
Through all of life's journey, there is just one thing I know.
That God has his purpose, and God has his plan.
And all that we have comes from his mighty hand.
Without him we are nothing, and life has no reason.
That he gives each life, its time, and its season.
The days may be many, or the days may be few.
But each one is a gift that he has given to you.
So forgive one another, and remember that he,
Forgave all your sins on Mt. Calvary.
The past is the past so help one another.
God made the bonds that bind you to your brother.
For someday you'll stand at the gates up above.
Where no one can enter without forgiving in love.
So live for each other and someone else too.
Life's not about *ours*, and it's not about *you*.
It's not about getting but giving away.
It's all about love and a debt to repay.
For things are never to keep, God gives them on loan.
Things are only to share and never to own.
The blessings he gives us are only to share.
To help someone else and lovingly care.
So open your heart and let his love flow.
For his love has held us together and allowed us to grow.
God has given us freely and abundantly too.
So put his love first in all that you do.
In all he has given, he wants us to know.
He holds us all counted and we reap what we sow.
So sow your seeds wisely, with love when you do.
For love never fails; love is strongest and true.

Love is all I can leave you; love will only remain.
But it's all that you need till I see you again.
It's all that I've lived for its all I can do.
It's forever and ever, and I'll always love you.
So keep our love living, hold it tight in your heart.
For in love is the victory, and we'll never part.
Know that I'm waiting; there's a new home above.
Keeping us once more together living in love.

After the Storm

Oh, the calm after the storm, the peace that follows the rain
The sweetness of the silence as stillness returns to earth again
The heavens now are quiet, a soft breeze blows sweetly from above
Showing me in the quiet God always sends his love
To shield me and protect me beneath his mighty arm
No power can overtake me or cause me any harm
Oh, let me praise and thank you, to serve you every day.
For the privilege of knowing you are with me, all along the way
Then once again when storms return, as storms will always do
When all the sky is dark and black, and no light is shining through
God help my trembling heart remember,
make my fearful mind maintain
Your promise that calm will follow the storm,
and peace will follow the rain

A Sudden Storm

As I was drifting on life's seas, a storm cloud ripped my sky
The lightning flashed and tossed me; my soul began to cry.

There wasn't any warning; there was no way to tell
This storm that now consumed, me right from the gates of hell.

The darkness took me under; I could not see the day
The angry waves engulfed me, and night had come to stay.

My God, why can't you see me; my God, are you still there
My God, I cannot find you; my God, do you still care?

The deepest hurt I'd ever known to this seemed smaller still
I can't seem to find my pathway that leads to Calvary hill.

I can't find my way, Lord; I'm groping in the night
I can't even feel your presence; are you hiding from my sight?

On my bed of confusion, I toss and I turn,
Has the candle gone out, does love flame really burn?

Then deep in my heart, far below all my feelings
My whole soul is sick, and my conscience mind reeling.

Yes, there in the ashes of my broken heart
Was the tiniest flicker that was not torn apart.

Slowly but surely, the flame catches hold
While the charred blackened ashes, slowly turned gold.

So ride out your darkness; storms never last
There pass on in God's time, regardless of the task.

For the Father says, it comes to pass; it doesn't come to stay
That he alone controls the storms that happen on our way.

That he controls the night times, regardless of how long
That he restores the daylight that brings the morning song.

There can never be nighttime, or a valley deep and wide
That will stop his flowing water, or still his healing tide.

It flows from Calvary's mountain down to every sinner's heart
With love and peace forever never to depart.

For he is the light forever, the one eternal flame
The master of the sea and precious is his name.

Jesus!

Summer '98

(Why We Love the Ocean)

When I went down to the seashore, I was burdened with care.
The hurts and all the heartaches seemed more than I could bear.
Yet deep within my being, I heard the spirit soft and true.
God said to me:

"Come, child, to the seashore; there waits my gift for you.
When I created all creation, I made the ocean carefully.
So when you come before it, you'll be coming close to me.
That's why I made the water soothing I sifted softness in the sand.
So when you walk upon it, you could easily understand.
That of all things whether large or small, above or beneath the sea.
It's you, my child, I treasure first, you mean the most to me.
So toss your troubles to the tide, your worries to the sea.
The ever-flowing ocean will bring them all to me.
As you watch the water wash them away beyond the endless shore.
You'll feel my love engulf you; the hurts are gone forever more.
So cast your cares upon me and send a dream or two.
For if you truly trust me, I'll make your dreams come true.
My spirit calms the water of the ocean vast and blue,
My spirit calms your troubled heart; I care so much for you.
That's why I made the ocean a place of peace, refreshing ever new.
So you will know that nothing of this world can love you like I do."

God's Love

If you took all the water from the crystal sea,
The mighty ocean would never be.

If you took all the sand from the endless shore,
The beautiful beach would be no more.

If you took the moon and the stars from the night,
There would be a pitch-black world without any light.

If you took the sun away from the day,
There would be no sunshine to brighten our way.

Your love is in all creation; your love is in every life.
Your love is in every triumph; your love is in every strife.

If you should take your eyes off me,
I'd be forever blind, and I could not see.

But if you took your love away from me,
My life and my soul would cease to be.

To Every Soldier

I don't know you from a photograph, a number or a name.
I know it doesn't matter; I know you just the same.
I never heard you on my radio, or saw you on TV
I don't know even where you are, but you are near and dear to me.
I wouldn't know you if we'd ever chance to meet.
I wouldn't recognize you either, if you walked across my street.
Still in my heart there is a place where only you can live.
Forever and for always for the sacrifice you give.
Your service and your honor so that I may live so free.
Are the reasons that I love you for the gift you give to me.
I'm so grateful and so thankful to our father up above.
Who created you, the soldier, that I don't know, but that I love.

A Memory on Mother's Day

A beautiful rose in a crystal vase could never measure up,
To the beauty I saw in a dandelion, stuffed in a paper cup.
A pretty strange picture you ask; how can that be?
A very rare portrait, drawn on a mother's memory.
I remember hearing whispers, and sounds of pure delight
And little boxes all wrapped up, and hidden out of sight.
I remember shiny breakfast trays, that surprised me on my bed,
And little ones with tender eyes, and tousled curly heads.
If all the cards at Hallmark were only mine to share,
I'd keep the ones smeared with pasty paste,
but made with loving care.
And all the world's jewels so costly and
rare could never begin to mean
As much to me as the jewels they gave, out of an old gum machine.
And if all the flowers in all the earth's gardens were given to me
Their beauty and splendor I'd fail to see.
Yes, if all the worlds worth could be all totaled up.
It couldn't measure the worth of the dandelion stuffed in the cup.
If I could only turn back time, if I could find a way.
To live again those precious times, and I could hear them say
"We love you, Mom. We really do. Happy Mother's Day!"
Of all the joys I've known, still the sweetest of my life,
Was when they called me "Mommy," and you called me "Wife."

To a Teenager from His Mother

My son so tall and handsome,
New manhood on your face,
I can't recall these passing years,
How fast we've run this race.
It was only yesterday, God placed you in our care,
Yet with love and happiness, time flies by; it seems to be unfair.
I know you want to hurry, find your place in world's gone mad,
But please for just a moment, wait and listen to your dad.
I know there are a million new things you must do,
But remember always in your mind; they're only new to you.
I know there are times you can't agree, and it's hard for you to see,
But it's not for now, or what you are, but what you're going to be.
He wants you to become a man, the man who stands apart,
Not one who grows just on the outside,
but who grows within his heart.
If I could only tell you how much he's given me,
Then it would be so simple, and you could easily see.
The value of the little things, to love, to think, to wait, to be fair.
To hope, to trust, to work, to care
To give to try, to want, to share.
For when you know these simple things, then
you'll stand straight and proud.
Pleasing to yourself, to us, and acceptable to God.
I want for you a thousand things, even some we've never had.
But most of all I want you to be just like your dad.
Then far out into tomorrow, I know that you'll be blessed.
To find a real love of your own and know her happiness.
Then off into that future, I know they'll be another little lad,
And a very special woman who prays he'll be just like his dad!

Mother's Love

(A Mother from Heaven)

I can no longer sing my song.
I can no longer tell you right from wrong.
The things undone I cannot do; I can no longer say.
I always tried to show you the straight and narrow way
The only thing I leave behind is of spirit strong and true
A heart that knew the love of God is the love I leave with you.
I've prayed for you my whole life through,
To give you only happiness I always tried to do.
I wanted each day full of sunshine, no dark clouds overhead
I wished you only happy days, never knowing any dread.
I wanted to protect you from any or all harm.
I wished I'd always hold you in the safety of my arms.
I tried to shield you every day so your heart would feel no fears
I wanted only joy to you, so your eyes would feel no tears
I tried to provide you with everything, a mother knows the need.
I loved you unconditionally, forgiving any deed.
I wanted the roads you walked to be smooth and easy along the way.
I wished you fun and happiness each and every day.
But life will always bring to us a dose of good and bad.
Sometimes we cannot control the things that make us sad.
But one thing sure you can depend on and learn to understand,
That everything and everyone God holds within his hands.
So seek him now and know his ways are always tried and true.
And he alone can do all things for you that I tried so hard to do.

On Father's Day

(From a Son in Heaven)

I know today is Father's Day; I know it's very hard
For you to bear the pain inside, or walk around the yard.
I'd like to hold you near me, so I'm sending you this card.
I just want to say I miss you; I just want you to know,
How very much I love you, and I see you there below.
But for this time and just right now, don't let your heart alarm,
I rest in God our Father, I'm safe from any harm.
I don't want you to worry, or let a day grow long,
Without my love around you, you'll always hear my song.
So look around the garden, watch the squirrels run up the trees,
Feel my warm kiss in the sunlight, my love on a gentle breeze.
See the sunrise in the morning, see the beauty of daytime bright,
See the sunset in the evening, the splendor of the night.
We're always watching over you; we're never very far,
We're just beyond the sunset, my home beyond a star.
It doesn't matter where or when; we'll never be apart.
You know we're real forever now; his love has filled your heart.
So forget about the little things we may have left undone,
You'll always be my father; I'll always be your son.
It really doesn't matter beyond this time and space,
All mistakes we humans make have vanished
through God's great grace.
I always knew you loved me; we always tried our best,
To do all things as we should, we didn't fail the test.
For dad, the greatest test in all the world I've won here up above,
It measures not in mark or grade; its score is endless love.

So on this Father's Day, please don't let me see you sad,
For always and forever, I'm so happy, proud, and glad.
That on the earth, I was the one allowed to call you "Dad."

But this heaven is a holy place; its beauty can't be spoken,
But best of all it is a place where our circle is unbroken.
So be assured that one day soon, in splendor and love,
God, the Father, will unite us in this heaven up above.

A Message from a Father in Heaven

It may seem I had to go too soon
It wasn't in our plan
But God, our Father, understood and issued that command
The work I left on earth below, God asks for you to do
He knows you are more than capable, and love will see you through
For sometimes, son, we only start, and may not get to see
Our work completes the battles won until eternity
God alone is sovereign; we cannot question why
Our partings are not known or time of last goodbyes
But one thing is sure: you can depend regardless of your loss
God gives us life eternal because of Calvary's cross
So take each day and do the work God has entrusted you
And know I'm watching proudly over everything you do
Though I had to leave you, I'm ever with you still
As you take over for me, my meager shoes to fill
And though I did not leave, a lofty wealth or fame
I left you all my love, my sons, my trust in Jesus's name
Someday soon, it won't be long, with angels standing guard
You'll be among the finest men, receiving that reward
For works, you did for me my son, for work you did with love
I'll be waiting oh so proudly, in our new home up above

Pastor

Lord, I want to thank you for our pastor, and may I ask of you
To give your guidance and protection, for all he has to do
For no one knows but you, Lord, the burdens that he bears
I'm sure the pastor sometimes wonders if anyone knows or cares

We often take for granted, forgetting he is human too
Often slight or inconsiderate of all he's going through
We expect him always humble, always at our call
When lots of times, it's our own lack, that causes us to fall

We expect him to solve our problems; give the answer that is right
Forgetting all the others who are not within our sight
We never see the sea of souls he prays for through the night
We never know or realize all the battles he must fight

For Satan knows the pastor is your chosen from above
That's why he attacks so much, the one who lives for love
Yes, Satan temps and tries, for he is everywhere
Can we stop the evil darts, if we cover the pastor with a prayer?

You see a pastor doesn't have a schedule;
no time clock checks him in
His shift is for a lifetime on a battlefield called sin
His body gets tired and weary; his mind needs peace and rest
Yet the pastor answers every call and always does his best

Help us remember he has a loving wife, often children of his own
He has many chores and things to do to make his house a home
Yet he spends his time with others, often leaving them alone

Then one day he sees through the eyes of
love, his little ones are grown
Yet no one complains or questions or asks why he wasn't there
To help them when they needed him, or had a special time to share

So forgive us, Lord, when we forget him who guides us every day
Teach us to follow wisely, supporting all the way
Keep us ever mindful of all we do and say
Let us know you'll hold us counted, on your coming judgment day
For he is our faithful pastor, our teacher, and our friend
He is the one who speaks to us, the message that you send

So thank you for this earthly shepherd, a gift from our Savior above
Please help us to follow both of you with gratitude and love

Drummondtown Community Church

Heavenly father, bless this church and all who enter in.
May all find your hope, your joy, your forgiveness of all sins.
May these walls keep the secrets of the many years long past.
May only the love and faith of our old members be all that last.
For, father God, this is your house; we pledge it always will remain.
A place of peace, a place of praise and worship
to bring honor to your name.
So help us, Lord; guide and teach us, Lord, in everything we do.
To be the church you call your own, we give all glory unto you.

Easter Sunday

(Sunrise Service)

As I stood alone at Easter, watched the sunrise on the sea.
I remembered all the other times you were standing there with me.
While we saw the splendor of creation displayed across the sky,
We swore our hearts together, vowed our love would never die.
We marveled at the ocean, gazed in wonder by the hour.
At its glory and its beauty, its mystery and its power.
It was here we watched the tides flow, saw the foam upon the blue.
It was here we first saw God and learned his word is true.
That he's the great creator of all the earth and the mighty sea.
That he created all the heavens in the
universe and even you and me.
We watched until the sunset, every seagull flying by.
Wondered could the Father really see us
from his home up in the sky.
Yes, our time spent at the seashore became a sacred part
Of all our love, our hopes, and dreams we carried in our hearts.
Now I'm here without you, yet I can hear you softly say,
"Remember, oh, remember, I have not gone away.
On this blessed Easter morning I want you most to know,
I wrap my love around you everywhere you go.
The love we shared is still the same and will forever be
Because I have seen our risen Savior, and he's won our victory.
So as you finish out life's tasks and do the Father's will,
Be assured of love forever as it conquered Calvary's hill.
Yes, hon, God is the great creator and holds
all things in his strong hand

"His grace and mercies endless, such love we cannot understand.
Yes, I clearly see you as our Father here above,
Who watches over all of us with eyes of purest love.
Yes, time spent at the ocean will always be a sacred thing
Because God's still the earth's provider and heaven's coming King.
So let us walk along the seashore, and our feet together in the sand.
I'll wrap my love around you; I'll always hold your hand.
Till I lead you safely into heaven you will never be alone,
You're just on a longer journey, hon, and
you'll soon be coming home."
So as I turn to leave the seashore, I know there is no choice.
I'll return again in wonder to let my thankful heart rejoice,
Singing praise to God our Father, who lets me hear your voice.

Thanksgiving

(First Thanksgiving without Your Loved One)

Father God, we thank you for everything you give
For everyone here, each precious and dear, and for
Every day that we live
But most of all, we thank you on this Thanksgiving Day
For the one we love ever so much, even though you have taken away
We know you're wise and wonderful in everything you do
We know that those you call are safely home with you
So help us, Lord, and teach us how we can go on living
So when you call to unite us all, we're prepared with
love and joy for an endless Thanksgiving!

Christmas

Please put Christ in Christmas, and let the children sing.
Of a little babe named Jesus and the God of everything.
For how can we remember if all we care to see,
Is Santa Claus and reindeer and tinsel on a tree.
We need to be reminded that all the gifts beneath the tree,
Are symbols of his wondrous love and the gift of Calvary.
For till we know this Jesus and all the peace he brings
Christmas is not Christmas or is not found in all the things.
For Christmas is a Christ child who came from God above.
To teach us all his goodness and teach us how to love.
For if we know about him, then we can learn to give.
To others all around us, and we will learn to live.
Then every day will be like Christmas, full of joy and love.
Because Christmas is God's greatest gift from heaven up above.

How Can I Have Christmas?

(First Christmas Without
Your Loved One)

How can I have Christmas when you're not here with me
How can I have Christmas, deck our halls or trim our tree
How can I remember the joy of ones gone by
Or see the yuletide beauty through eyes that only cry
How can I have Christmas because of Jesus's birth
How can I have Christmas because he came to earth
To show his light to all the world his peace and joy impart
Showing me that Christmas is the love within my heart
When I feel his presence, I can so clearly see
Together with us at Christmas, throughout eternity.

There'll Always Be a Song

There will always be a song in my heart that will never go away.
Its sweet sound comforts my darkest night and calms my lonely day.
The world around me cannot know or hear its gentle key,
It's a melody of memory that belongs to you and me.
The pain and all its sorrow that has overwhelmed my heart.
Has tried to still its tender song since death did make us part.
But no matter how deep my hurt the grief cannot erase,
The song of love within my heart that nothing can replace.
For though you are not with me, I love you even more.
I know you're waiting for me across the golden shore
So I can face tomorrow, I know that there will be
Another time, another place, we'll share our melody.
So as I remain, as God will lead you'll always be the part
That makes my battered soul rejoice and
keeps the song within my heart.

To Pap Rayner

Once there was a little girl who crawled on Grandpap's knee
They laughed and talked, and shared, as happy as could be.
They were always buddies and always had such fun
From early in the morning to the setting of the sun.
Now a pap is very special; he knows a thousand things
He knows about the moon and stars and what makes an angel sing.
He knows about a robin, the forest, and the trees.
He knows about dogwood and even honey bees.
He knows about a woodchuck, with a hollow in the ground.
He knows about the wheel, and why it turns around.
Why paps are great to talk to, and with a secret share
He'll have the time to listen, and have the time to care.
Not only if you're little, but even if you've grown.
You know you can depend on him, you are never on your own.
Our lives may change; we rearrange ourselves from place to place.
But all the love he's shown us never changes face.
The years have passed the child has grown
But all the things remain inside, just as the seeds were sown.
Yes, paps are really special; we could never count the ways
He's always stood behind us and brightened up our days.
I know that God protects him, and watches from above
And lets him stay still with us, and fill our world with love.
I just want to say I love you, thanks for all you do.
I know there's not another pap, in all the world like you!

My Prayer for Pappy Lennox

(for One with Alzheimer's Disease)

Help me, Lord, to care for one, who one time cared for me.
To do the tasks that must be done, with love and dignity.
Help me, Lord, to give to him, as he once gave to me.
All the things that he needs now, whatever they may be.

Show me, Lord, your way to do whatever I must do.
To know as his strength goes, I'll find my strength in you.
Now little things he used to do, to me he must surrender.
Lord, give me strength and wisdom; make
me always kind and tender.
To answer all the questions, though repeated they may be.
Make my answers soft and kindly and thought out carefully.

For now, his steps are staggered, and his voice is weak and low.
And simple things if asked of him, he simply doesn't know.
Let me put a little sunshine into his lonely day.
To cause a smile to cross his face, as we go along this way.
For him, it can't be easy yet I hear him not complain.
But I hear him often whisper a prayer in Jesus's name.

Yes, the body fails us quickly, as age changes every part.
But thanks to God our Father it can never change the heart.
And when I can't be with him, Lord, I know that you will send.
A band of heaven's angels, to his every need attend.
So help me, Lord, to do the best for him regardless of the test.
Until you call him safely home, to his eternal rest.

To Mammaw and Pappy

(To Grandparents)

From childhood to manhood, there was never a day
That you didn't help us in some special way
You made every day a wondrous thing,
You showed us a bird's nest, said why robins sing.
You taught us to count and read from a book,
That God's all around us wherever we look.
Mammaw taught us hide-and-seek, and how to blow our noses,
Pappy taught us little boys should learn to love the roses.
Mammaw baked us cookies and taught us how to snap our buckles.
Pappy taught us to make a fist, and how to crack our knuckles.
Mammaw said to be polite and look after little brother.
Pappy said to stand up tall, to love our dad and mother
Mammaw said to be good in school, and
remember right from wrong.
Pappy said that being rough was not the same as being strong.
From bumps on our heads to scratches on our knees,
From catching a butterfly or climbing up trees,
It was Mammaw and Pappy who dried up the tears,
Or turned on the light that chased away fears.
They made every birthday a party, each one in a row,
Full of laughter and fun, and candles to blow.
Each Christmas was magic, with memories we treasure,
Toys and surprises, made a year full of pleasure.
But behind all the giving and sharing delight,
We learned about Jesus and a Bethlehem night.
Yes, from snowmen in winter, to days at the beach.

They showed us the Heavens, and the stars we could reach.
We have been the lucky kids; we're blessed in every way,
Our future path is clear now; love will light our way.
We know we will make it; we must and we can,
That love is the measure and worth of a man.
We'll follow the course; the way you have shown,
You won't have to worry or wonder, we've grown.
We know how to do it; we'll make you proud and happy.
We'll just have to be like our Mammaw and Pappy.

God Made Great Beauty

God made great beauty in the heavens
God made great beauty in the seas
God made great beauty in the earth, the forest, and the trees.
He made great beauty all around us and made us eyes to see.
The greatest beauty, of the heart, he placed in you and me.

To All Mothers

In all the world, there is not one single word that means love more than Mother. Regardless of country, creed, religion, origin, or language, Mother is love, and love is Mother. Whoever you may be, if you are called Mother, Mom, Momma, Mommy, Stepmother, Godmother, or special adoptive Mother, you are special. If you are called Grandma, Grammy, Great-Grandma, Nanny or Mee-Maw, Auntie, or special friend, you share love in many ways. Whatever you may be, married, divorced, widowed, or a single mom on your own, you are part of a sisterhood that God himself created and called motherhood. Regardless of who you are, where you are, or what you may be experiencing right now, we are all bonded in love. Mothers everywhere know and share your sacrifices and struggles. The role of a mother is both rewarding and challenging. It's a lifelong journey no matter what age you may be. To mothers everywhere, you are admired, you are respected, you are deserving, you are appreciated, you are remembered, you are celebrated, you are special, and you are loved. Happy Mother's Day to all who wear the name of mother and wear the badge of love and courage called motherhood. God bless you all! Happy Mother's Day.

Young Love

When we were so young, and our love was so new
My heart was so sure, I'd always love you
With a smile so sweet and a kiss so tender
The love in your eyes caused my total surrender

Our new world was so precious, in wonderment grew
My happiness complete was all wrapped up in you
Our hearts beat together, our thoughts were as one.
Just as natural as tides flow, the rise of the sun.

You were always beside me, my strength and my guide
No words can describe, and our hearts filled with pride
As our love just kept growing, all boundaries outgrew
As time added years, our love stayed ever-fresh ever new.

We knew all the passion, we felt all the pain
We knew times of heartache and shared all the gains.

We fought all the battles life pushed in our way
With courage and love as God showed us each day
To hang on to each other and his face to seek
That he was all strong when we were so weak.

Love gave us moments too sacred to share
Our times together, when our souls were made bare
It didn't seem strange to you or me
It was always so simple, just meant to be

Our love was our reason and each of us knew
It wasn't our doing, to us was no due
Even in struggle or time of despair
The love always held us the load we could bear.

For our life together seemed blessed and rare
And nothing around us seemed to compare

Regardless of troubles or problems or strife
True love is the gift from the giver of life
For God in his wisdom created it so
That when sharing true love causes each one to know
The love of the Father, the gift of the Son
The miracle of life is when two become one.

You're the Reason

The happiness you've brought to me
There are no words to say
The joy I've shared with you, the
The love we've known each day.

You're the reason I get up,
You're the reason I lay down
You're the reason my heart smiles
You're the reason I can't frown.

You're the greatest gift I've ever had
You're my gift from God above
You're the reason I am happy
You're the reason that I love.

I thank the good Lord up above
For only he could see
How very much I love and need you
You're everything to me.

The love I feel for you no one but God could give
You're my one and only treasure
You're the reason that I live
Your precious, kind, and loving
You're thoughtful strong and true
My love for you is endless
Forever and for always
My one and only you.

I love you so much!

Anniversary

(Suzanne and Kevin)

Our journey has been sometimes tough, the path a little rough.
But through it all; our love remains and has always been enough.
To get us through the hard times, and times we now recall.
The times we may have stumbled, but times we did not fall.
We laughed, we loved, we danced, whatever came our way.
We kept our hearts together, and we can truly say,
That we'll always love each other, no matter what will be.
God made us truly soul mates, for all eternity.
For marriage is a bond we know, a vow not to be broken.
For God above declares it so, and his word had spoken.
So I thank you for the happy years and the love you've given me.
Without your smile and tender touch, how hopeless life would be?
So we'll keep our hearts together and pray to God above.
To guide us and protect us and keep us in his love.

New Baby

Some say, that it will never be, that man will never see.
The Son of God, upon this earth, till dawns the time, eternity
But there is a time, I know it's true; he visits us below
In weather fair, or blizzard rare, or when it rains or snows.
For everyone who has the name "Mother," surely knows
Oh, not to just a special few but each and every one
With every woman, everywhere, who births a daughter or a son
He gently hovers over them and softly calms her fears
Or doubts. Unknown, he clears heart and
mind with cleansing loving tears
Oh, when you say the edge of night or in the early morn?
The time is told he comes, back here, each time a child is born
Oh yes, he does return, for each and every
birth and he patiently stands by
Till life is safe, each heartbeat calm, but the biggest reason why,
God comes below, he has to know, his spirit will not fly,
Away from them until he hears,
Each precious newborn cry. Amen.

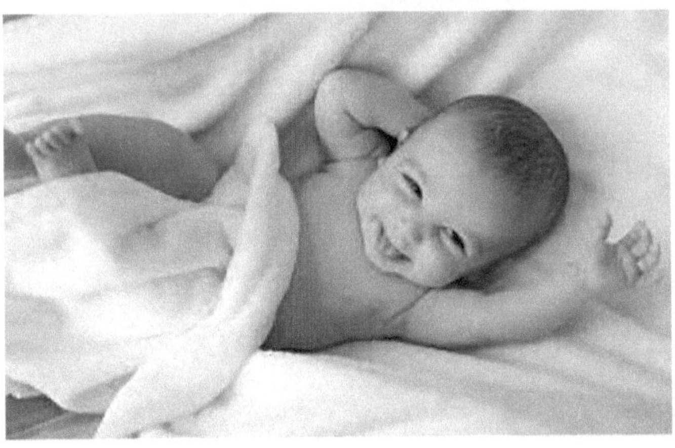

Little Cottage

Oh, little cottage, down by the sea
Filled with peace and serenity,
Filled with joy and hope and love,
Built to glorify God above.

So all who enter will find peace and rest
In him whose love is true and best.
So when they leave, these walls depart,
Find them filled with joy and a softer heart.

Then its purpose is granted and will always be
Sharing God's love in this little cottage
Down by the sea.

Blessing

Thank you, God, for another day,
Your wondrous blessing I see
But thank you, God, most of all,
For the blessing that sleeps next to me.

Garter

With lots of love, we give to you
This little garter trimmed in blue
We thank our Father up above
Who gives to all the gift of love?

Seamstress

(Linda)

We know our seamstress is a gift from heaven up above.
God placed her here to show us all, his gift of endless love.
She sews his hope in every hem; his love attaches each piece of lace.
Her award, for now, is the smile she sees, on each and every face.
There are yards and yards of fabric, only she can safely measure.
She sews so carefully because she knows
it's someone's special treasure.
Every button is sewn, every tiny bead is
placed, exactly where it should be.
The thread is delicate and fragile, almost impossible to see.
Little do the people know the endless hours she spends.
Sewing, stitching, threading, while days and night times end.
Her eyes get tired, her fingers get very sore.
Her list will never end, it's always "Just one dress more."
She never complains or questions what we ask her to do.
She is always faithful and loyal, honest and true.
She is the one that we depend on; she'll go the extra mile.
Her agreement is always willing; her answer is a smile.
We all love her dearly; we know we can't repay.
The many times she helps us, each and every day.
She accomplishes every task and will always do her part
To complete the work, she started with her
hands but finished with her heart.

Music Lessons

He couldn't hit the ball so well; he never made the hit.
He always tried to run in the track but couldn't really make it.
His spelling wasn't very great, and his math was really sad.
He used to think what can I do if all I do turns bad.
Then Mr. Nutter came to school; he's the leader of the band.
The talk he gave, the things he said, really sounded grand.
He listened to the kids that played; they sounded very well.
If he could be a part of that, wouldn't that be swell?
He raised his hand and signed his name. He was all set to try.
That shining horn with all the knobs his parents had to buy.
He blew and blew; he tried so hard; he practiced very long,
Until one day the noise he made sounded something like a song.
He was a little scratchy, maybe just a bit too loud,
But to his ears, it sounded sweet, and he was very proud.
At last, he'd found a place to fit, a place where he could be,
A part of something very good that all his friends could see.
He liked himself; he learned to care.
He learned to hear the music as he learned to work and share.
Now Mr. Nutter teaches many things we could never measure.
The hours of work and endless days of memories to treasure.
But most of all and best to say, the things that stand above,
Aren't lessons taught in note or scale but lessons taught in love.

A Queen without a Crown

(Young Teen Cancer Patient)

There was no crown upon her head,
There wasn't even hair.
Somehow, I didn't notice,
I just envisioned it was there.
Her face was softly radiant
Her presence filled the air.
I sensed her gentle spirit the instant she was there.

Her eyes told me a story; there were no words to say.
Immediately I loved her in a very special way.
Her beauty seemed to fill the room,
We talked for just a while
Right away she stole my heart,
With the sweetness in her smile.

Somehow, she was soft and fragile,
Delicate pure and true.
Yet she was sure and solid,
Strong from all the struggle she'd been through

Real beauty isn't crowns of gold or golden locks of hair.
Real beauty comes from within a heart
That has suffered deep despair.
A heart that feels true loneliness, but never lets you know.
A heart that has known fear and pain,
But never lets it show.

My heart cries out to heaven; Father, hear my prayer.
Keep her close to you, Lord; wrap her in your care.

I know we should not question what we cannot understand.
That every life is God's alone and that you hold each hand.

I know that you are with her I see it on her face.
I feel your love surround her with your amazing grace.

She's the bravest little soldier, that there could ever be.
She's the most beautiful of queens, that I will ever see.

Yes, she touched my life; she changed my
life; she turned it upside down.
This pretty little queen that doesn't wear a crown.

To Louie

You're always part of my purpose
You're always part of my plan.
You're always the one that I reach for when I need a hand.
You've shown me to face calmly, the tensions and worry.
You have told me there are always two sides to a story.
You're brave and fearless when I feel so weak.
You've shown me when to be quiet and when I should speak.
You've told me that morning will always follow the night.
That darkness can't stay if we follow the light.
You lead me and teach me you show me the way.
To make sunshine and peace a part of each day.
I am humbled and honored to call you my friend.
This bond that we share can't break or end.
I am grateful and thankful to God up above.
Who gave us each other, our time, and our love?

I Wonder

I often lay alone at night and wonder what I'll do.
When my time comes to go, can I make it
over or will I make it through?
Will I be sick or all alone, or will I be in pain?
Is there truly life again, and will it be my gain?
Is there a place called heaven? Is there a place called hell?
The greatest of life's mysteries no one can ever tell.

I think we do not know the day we're born, or know the day we die.
These things belong to God above who knows the reasons why.
But so many questions all unanswered,
just too much to comprehend.
As I think of past and present, the beginning and the end.

Yes, to think is very human, but to love is most divine.
For love is what God gave us, that has stood the test of time.
Then I think of Jesus, I see that sacred cross.
I think of all that he went through, that love is never lost.

I think, what kind of love could make him die for me.
What kind of love would hold him there to suffer on that tree?
This kind of love can't be explained; it's the greatest mystery
Than any of life's little questions, that seem to puzzle me.
Then I recall the many times, when there was "nothing I could do"
I called on the name of Jesus, and he gave me life anew.

Then suddenly my heart sees very clearly,
what my mind and eyes can't see.
That wondrous love is all I need to face eternity.
That love is all that matters, the love of Jesus strong and true.
I know his love will take me over, and his love will take me through.

It's Time

It's time to come to Jesus; do not wait another day
It's time to ask forgiveness; it's time for us to pray
It's time to take the Bible down that sits upon the shelf
It's time to love each other and forget about yourself
It's time to know you cannot linger; there is no time to wait
It's time to know you have a choice; do not pause or hesitate
It's time to think about time, when time will be no more
It's time to learn about the Savior who is waiting at the door
It's time to love your neighbor; it's time to be a friend
It's time to know all time is measured; it's
time to know that time will end
It's time to know the Savior who sees all things from up above
He sees his world so shattered and so lacking in his love
It's time now to accept his love, ask him into your broken heart
It's time to love forever; he'll always do his part
He'll keep you and protect you wherever you may tread
You're safe in him forever; he is the Son of God
It's time now; he is gathering all in heaven, the saints and angels too
It's time he is coming for all his children,
and that means me and you
He knows the world has lost his rhythm; he
knows this world has lost his rhyme.
So he waits till God, his Father, will tell him when it's time.

Much is written regarding weddings, brides, and love. However, long after vows are taken what really happens to the love? Does it get better, does it endure, does it end? Let me tell you what I know. I know it does get better; it does endure, because love, true love, never ends. Since love is a gift, God's greatest gift to all humanity, also all creation. We must know the giver of this awesome gift before we can ever learn to love one another. As we share those vows, "For better or worse, in sickness and in health, for richer or for poorer." Even the storms of life cannot change it because love is the anchor, and the anchor holds. It is not easy to ever imagine facing life without that one person, who makes you so complete. Love and life are still facts we must all face, one day. I can only tell you my story. I know even death does not destroy it, or even change it. I can only tell you for sure that love lives in my heart. I still have the joy and the wonder of love. I was only eighteen years of age in 1957 when we shared our vows, and as I now face my eighty-fifth year, I can only assure you it's still the same. I am by definition a widow. I cannot relate to or address the term *widow* because I am still his wife, Mrs. Herman Lennox. I thank God, every day for him, for the blessings I have known. Love never fails! Thank you for allowing me to share. I've enclosed a few poems that I feel helped me to reach this day, and by sharing maybe someone is facing the hardest part of their lives. It may help them know they too will endure because *true love never fails and love never ends*!

Thank you.

Sincerely,
Mrs. Lennox

About the Author

Herk and Marlene Lennox

A true love story transpired and touched the lives of so many. If you know Marlene, you know just how special love is to her. She married her high school sweetheart, built a family, and then built an amazing business (Lennox East). Through every stage of life and every obstacle, the foundation was love. She often says, "A woman in love can do anything," and I firmly believe that is true. Love brings out the best in us and makes us stronger.

Lennox East is one of Maryland's oldest and most distinguished bridal formal wear stores. Established in 1979, Lennox East has enjoyed forty-two years in the business of serving customer who looks for unique and beautiful things. Lennox East has dressed countless national winners for Maryland and surrounding states. It has gained a solid reputation in the area for prom and pageant gowns.

Lennox East is also known for its tradition of beautiful and elegant weddings. Nothing compares to the style and service Lennox East devotes to each bride. This is a very special store

devoted to you and your wedding. Lennox East has been chosen as one of the top 200 bridal stores in the United States. Marlene always says, "The Store Runs on A Lot of Love and a Whole Lot of Chocolate."

Comptroller Award

Best Bridal on the Beach

Lennox East has been awarded numerous awards over the years.